Understanding Neglect

A Book for
Young Children

By Beth Richey, LCSW, RPT-S & Paula Wood, LCSW

ISBN: 978-1-954614-52-9 (hard cover)
        978-1-954614-46-8 (soft cover)

Editing: Amy Ashby

Warren
publishing

Published by Warren Publishing
Charlotte, NC
www.warrenpublishing.net
Printed in the United States

Dedicated to all the healers at Gemma Services

All kids are **lovable** and deserve to be *safe* and *cared for*.

Grown-ups are in charge of making sure kids have **everything** they need to *grow* up safe, healthy, and happy.

There are rules and laws about the things grown-ups **NEED** to give kids. The rules are that kids need:

Food: Children should have enough food every day so they don't feel too hungry and their bodies can be healthy and strong.

A HOME: Children need a place to live where it is warm in the winter, and there is clean water to drink and electricity for lights. And children shouldn't have to keep moving to a lot of different places.

SCHOOL: Kids need to go to school every day to learn important things like numbers and math, letters and reading.

SUPERVISION: A grown-up or teenager needs to be with children at all times. Kids should never be left alone in the home or with someone who is too young.

BODY CARE: It's important for children to go to the doctor and dentist to be healthy, and grown-ups need to make sure children have clean bodies and clothing.

SAFETY: Children need to be protected from unsafe people and situations where kids could get hurt.

LOVE: Grown-ups should use kind words
and help children feel special and wanted.

When children don't have these things, it's a problem, and *special helpers* come in to help the grown-ups with what is missing.

Sometimes children are brought to a *new home*, called a foster home, while their grown-up tries to fix the problems.

Some grown-ups can fix the problems and learn how to give kids everything they need. Then the kids can go back home where they can *grow* and *learn*, and be safe and **happy**.

Some grown-ups are not able to learn how to give kids all the things they need.
Then kids have to stay in the new home with a **grown-up** who can.

There are lots of reasons why this might be, but
it is **never** the child's fault.

You are **special**. You are lovable.
You deserve to have *everything* you need.

About this book:

This book is written for young children to help them understand the difficult topic of neglect, and what children need and deserve. Written in a simple and straightforward manner, it enables children to make better sense of what "neglect" means, and why they were removed from their homes. It is intended for professional use by trained clinicians specializing in therapy with children.

For Therapists:

This book can be read alone or with a trusted caregiver in the therapy space. See the below sample questions that can be used to accompany this book.

- Tell me some ways you are lovable. What are good things about you?
- What are some examples of things kids need?
- What were some things in your home you did you not have enough of?
- What are your feelings about what kids need?
- What are your feelings about living in a new home?
- Whose fault do you think it is that your caregiver was not able to give you everything you need?
- Can you still love the grown-up who did not give you all the things you need?
- Who is the grown-up who gives you all the things you need now?

About the Authors:

Paula is a nationally certified Trauma Focused-Cognitive Behavioral Therapist in Philadelphia, Pennsylvania where she provides counseling services to children and their families. She is trained in EMDR, Parent Child Interaction Therapy, and Play Therapy. She enjoys kayaking and playing with her mischievous cats.

Beth is a play and trauma therapist in Philadelphia, Pennsylvania. She is nationally certified in Trauma Focused-Cognitive Behavioral Therapy and has training in the areas of Parent Child Interaction Therapy, Family Therapy, and Play Therapy. She has published the *Trauma Reaction Cards for Children and Adolescents* and *Me Magnets: An Identity and Self-Expression Tool.* Beth enjoys crafting and playing with her house full of pets.

www.ingramcontent.com/pod-product-compliance
Lightning Source LLC
Chambersburg PA
CBHW041432040426
42445CB00021B/1988